FORMULA 1

Paul Mason

amicus
mankato, minnesota

Published by Amicus
P.O. Box 1329, Mankato, Minnesota 56002

Planning and production by
Tall Tree Limited
Editor: Rob Colson
Designer: Jonathan Vipond

Printed in the United States of America by
Bang Printing, Brainerd, Minnesota.

Published by arrangement with the Watts
Publishing Group Ltd., London.

Library of Congress Cataloging-in-Publication Data
Mason, Paul.
  Formula 1 / by Paul Mason.
     p. cm. -- (Motorsports)
  Includes index.
  Summary: "Explains the history of Formula 1
racing and the how-to of the sport"--Provided by
publisher.
  ISBN 978-1-60753-117-3 (library binding)
  1. Grand Prix racing--Juvenile literature. 2.
Formula one automobiles--Juvenile literature. I.
Title.
  GV1029.15.M37 2011
  796.72--dc22
                                    2009033531

1208
32010

9 8 7 6 5 4 3 2 1

Picture credits:
BMW AG: 6, 10, 11, 12 bottom, 13, 18 middle, 23,
26, 29 middle left, 29 bottom right.
Corbis: 9 bottom (Schlegelmilch), 16
(Schlegelmilch), 24 bottom (Schlegelmilch), 27
(China Photos/Reuters).
Dreamstime: cover middle (Afby71), cover bottom
left (Chris Nolan), cover bottom middle (Afby71),
cover bottom right (Shaiful Rizal Mohd Jaafar), 3
(Afby71), 13 middle right (Davejob), 14–15
(Afby71), 15 bottom right (Andrea Presazzi), 29
top left (Afby71).
Getty Images: 7 (AFP), 8 (Hulton Getty collection),
9 top (Popperfoto), 17 middle left (AFP), 17 right,
19, 20–21, 24–25, 29 bottom left, 29 top right.
iStockphoto: 18 top and bottom (ptilley).
Mark McArdle/GNU: 15 top right, 29 right middle
Morio/GNU: 22
Shell Motorsport: 12–13

Every attempt has been made to clear copyright.
Should there be any inadvertent omission, please
apply to the publisher for rectification.

CONTENTS

THE BIGGEST PRIZE

A man dangles a sign by the side of the track. It reads: "Massa +1.7." Lewis Hamilton's McLaren howls past in a blur, followed a heartbeat later by the red Ferrari of rival Felipe Massa. Blink and you'll miss them.

Welcome to the heat of battle in a Formula 1 race.

A POPULAR MOTORSPORT

Formula 1 is the world's most popular motorsport championship. The races are most popular in Europe and Asia. Grand Prix races in the United States were canceled in 2008 and in Canada in 2009. Many factors, such as the economy, went into these decisions.

△ *Felipe Massa, in a Ferrari, leads Lewis Hamilton's McLaren through the first corner of the Turkish* **Grand Prix**.

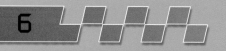

RACING AROUND THE WORLD

Formula 1 races are known as Grand Prix, which is French for "big prize." Teams and drivers compete against each other in a season that consists of up to 18 Grand Prix. Some races, such as Monaco, take place on closed roads. Most, however, are held on purpose-built tracks.

A SEASON OF RACING

The Formula 1 season lasts from spring until late autumn. The drivers and teams are awarded points according to where they finish in each race. At the end of the season, the points are added up to decide the champion driver and team. In 2008, after a nail-biting final race in Brazil, Lewis Hamilton of the United Kingdom won the Drivers' Championship, and Italian team Ferrari was the leading team.

▽ *British driver Lewis Hamilton celebrates victory in the 2008 Chinese Grand Prix, one of the five races he won on the way to clinching the 2008 Drivers' Championship.*

EARLY DAYS OF FORMULA 1

The first Grand Prix drivers were daredevils. They raced in cars without any safety features and crashes were often fatal. Between 1954 and 1994, 27 Formula 1 drivers died in crashes. Cars are now much safer and no driver has been killed since 1994.

EARLY MOTOR RACING

Early motor races were held on public roads. Watching was almost as dangerous as driving. Many **spectators** were killed in crashes. In the early 1900s, the authorities decided that racing should only be allowed on **closed circuits**, and Grand Prix racing was born.

◁ Early races, such as this one in Scotland in 1908, often went right through towns.

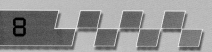

THE FANGIO ERA

The first Formula 1 championship was held in 1950. One driver soon dominated: Juan Manuel Fangio. The Argentine driver won the world championship in 1951 and every year from 1954 to 1957. Fangio's battles with drivers such as Britain's Stirling Moss made Formula 1 increasingly popular.

△ *Juan Manuel Fangio, in car 18, races alongside German rival Karl Kling. Both are driving Mercedes cars in the 1954 French Grand Prix.*

TECHNICAL DATA

In 1971, Peter Gethin won the Italian Grand Prix with an average speed of 150.754 mph (242.615 km/h). It was the fastest Grand Prix ever.

THE LOTUS YEARS

During the 1960s, a new power dominated Formula 1: the British Lotus team. Lotus used revolutionary materials and **aerodynamics** to gain an edge on other teams. Ever since, **technology** has been crucial to success in Formula 1.

▽ *By 1969, car design had moved on, as Graham Hill's Lotus shows.*

THE TEAM

Each team has two racing drivers. They are the ones who will stand on the podium if they come first, second, or third. But any driver will admit that winning, or even racing, would be impossible without his team.

DESIGNING A CAR

A Formula 1 team's **engineers** start work on their new season's car months before the racing begins. Once the racing is underway, they continue making changes. They constantly **analyze** and modify the car to improve its performance.

Nose

△ A CAD (Computer-Aided Design) for the nose and front wing of the BMW Sauber Formula 1 car.

Front wing

TEST DRIVERS

Once a car has been developed, the test drivers get their hands on it. Their job is to drive thousands of miles at **race pace**. The information the team gets from testing helps to improve the car's speed, handling, and **reliability**.

△ BMW Sauber test driver Christian Klien (in the car) chats with driver Nick Heidfeld (right).

MECHANICS

Mechanics travel to each Grand Prix with the drivers. If the car is damaged in practice or during the race, it is their job to repair it. If the driver crashes in practice, the mechanics may have to rebuild the car overnight!

TECHNICAL DATA

Formula 1's rules say that no team can do more than 18,641 mi. (30,000 km) of seasonal testing. That's far enough to drive three-quarters of the way around the world.

THE CAR: SPEEDING UP— AND SLOWING DOWN

The top speed of a Formula 1 car is about 198 mph (320 km/h). How do the cars get up to such high speeds? Just as importantly, how are they able to slow down quickly enough to get around corners?

Rear wing

TECHNICAL DATA

Formula 1 engines suck in 650 liters of air a second! They travel just 0.8 mi. (1.3 km) on ¼ gallon (1 L) of fuel.

▷ *The Ferrari car driven by Brazilian Felipe Massa.*

GO POWER

Formula 1 cars have 2.4 liter engines—smaller than some ordinary family cars. Even so, they produce power of well over 600 **bhp**. A normal car has about 100 bhp of power. Imagine a tug-of-war between the two!

AERODYNAMICS

Aerodynamics describes the way a moving object travels through the air. Formula 1 cars are designed to be able to travel through the air as easily as possible. This allows them to reach the highest speeds and gives them the best **fuel consumption**.

◁ *A computer simulation shows how air flows over a Formula 1 car traveling at high speed.*

STOP POWER

Formula 1 cars stop when two pads grip a brake disc attached to each wheel. Sometimes the cars brake so hard that their discs glow yellow-hot. Brake discs for normal races are made of **carbon fiber**. In wet races, steel discs allow the pads more grip.

Brake disc

Front wing

13

THE CAR: GRIP

Formula 1 cars corner at speeds well over 124 mph (200 km/h). That's so fast that the drivers need a special harness to keep them from being thrown out of their seats. How do the cars grip the track so hard?

SUSPENSION

A car's suspension flexes up and down, keeping the tires in contact with the ground even over bumps and **curbs**. The suspension also absorbs some of the forces created when a car goes around corners.

▲ *The suspension on Vitantonio Liuzzi's Scuderia Toro Rosso car keeps it running smoothly over the curb.*

TECHNICAL DATA

Modern Formula 1 cars can generate grip that would hold 3.5 times their own weight. In theory, they could be driven upside down!

▷ If drivers take corners too quickly, the rear wheels may not grip the track surface enough and the rear of the car slides out. This is known as oversteer and can cause a car to spin out of control.

AIRFLOW AND GRIP

Changing how air flows over a car affects its grip. On a twisty, slower racetrack, teams set up the airflow to push the car down hard, giving the tires more grip. On a fast, straight racetrack, they let the air flow smoothly over the car, giving it more speed.

Wet tires

Intermediate tires

TIRES

The car's tires are what hold the car to the track. Teams can choose between dry, wet, or intermediate tires, depending on the weather conditions. Dry tires, called "slicks," are smooth. Wet and intermediate tires are **grooved**.

WHITING, IN 46394

PRACTICE AND QUALIFYING

Formula 1 weekends start with a practice session. Next comes qualifying, which can be the most important part of the weekend. Qualifying times decide the drivers' order on the starting grid, where being at the front is a big advantage.

PRACTICE

Every Grand Prix driver's weekend starts with practice. During practice, the drivers get used to the circuit. At the same time, the teams make decisions about the best tires, suspension, and aerodynamics to use in qualifying.

QUALIFYING

During the early qualifying sessions, all the drivers try to record the fastest lap they can. The drivers who record the 10 fastest laps get to take part in the final qualifying session.

△ Lewis Hamilton crosses the finish line during qualifying at Indianapolis, Indiana.

FINAL QUALIFYING

In final qualifying, the fastest 10 drivers have a "shoot-out" to decide their grid positions for the start of the race. Each tries to set the fastest **flying lap**. Getting a good grid position is especially important on racetracks where overtaking is difficult, such as Hungary and Valencia.

▷ *Qualifying times decide who starts at the front of the grid for the actual race. The best place to start from is known as the* **pole position**.

△ *Former McLaren boss Ron Dennis keeps an eye on the progress of rival Ferrari teams during qualifying for the Belgian Grand Prix.*

Pole position

TECHNICAL DATA

At the 2008 Italian Grand Prix, Sebastian Vettel became the youngest driver ever to be on the pole position. At just 21 years old, Vettel then went on to win, making him the youngest-ever winner, too.

URNE AUSTRALIA ME

THE START

Drivers can gain several places on the other racers if they get off to a good start. Some drivers, such as Felipe Massa and Lewis Hamilton, are famous for fast starts.

WARM UP LAP

Before the actual start, all the cars do a "warm up lap." During the sighting lap the drivers weave across the track, accelerate, and brake hard, keeping their cars warmed up for the race.

◁ The green lights come on to signal the start of the sighting lap.

STARTING LIGHTS

After the warm up lap, the drivers line up on the grid. The starting lights begin to come on: one red, then two, three, four, five red lights show. When the lights go out, it's the signal to race away from the line!

▽ All the red start lights light up: when they go out, it's foot to the floor time.

Ready...

...get set...

...go!

△ Three red lights mean it's almost time to go at the Australian Grand Prix.

TECHNICAL DATA

It's not always impossible to win from the back. At the 1983 U.S. Grand Prix, John Watson started 22nd on the grid and finished first.

THE FIRST CORNER

Formula 1 cars have special "launch control" systems to help the drivers get a good start. Even so, some drivers always get off faster than others. Everyone wants to reach the first corner ahead of the pack!

△ *Felipe Massa loses control of his Ferrari at the first bend of the Australian Grand Prix. Only the drivers' lightning-quick reflexes prevent mass pileups when this happens.*

IN THE PIT LANE

During the race, the drivers have to stop to take on fuel and fresh tires. This means they have to pull into the pit lane for their pit crew to work on the car. Every member of the pit crew has an important job to do, as even a one or two second delay could cost the team victory.

FUEL CREW

The two men in the fuel crew have to handle a heavy refueling hose. They pump huge amounts of fuel into the car in under 10 seconds. Just enough fuel is added to get the car to its next stop (or the finish).

▶ *The Ferrari team gets to work on Felipe Massa's car as he makes a planned pit stop during a race.*

TECHNICAL DATA

The fastest-ever pit stop in Formula 1 took just 3.2 seconds! It happened in 1993, when Benetton driver Riccardo Patrese was given fresh tires.

LOLLIPOP MAN

The lollipop man is there to let the driver know what to do. He holds out a sign to keep the driver at a standstill. When the stop is almost over, he turns the lollipop around to warn the driver that he needs to be ready to leave.

TIRE CHANGERS

The tire changers actually change the whole wheel, not only the tires. For each wheel, one man works the nut gun, another whips off the wheel and tire, and a third replaces it. That's a crew of 12 just for the tire changes!

RACE STRATEGY

Teams can have the fastest car, the best drivers, and a brilliant pit crew, but still not win races. The reason is usually that something has gone wrong with their race strategy—the plans they made before the race started.

FUEL AND TIRES

Formula 1 cars have to stop during races to change tires and add fuel. Teams can make one, two, or even three stops. Making one stop saves time but also means the car will be slower. It is carrying more fuel and the tires have to last longer.

▽ *Nico Rosberg in a Williams racecar outbrakes Nick Heidfeld's BMW Sauber to overtake on the inside. There are very few places to overtake, so drivers must plan their moves carefully.*

PIT-STOP WINDOWS

Team "pit-stop windows" are the times in the race
when a pit stop must be made. For example, the
first window could be between lap 19 and 21. If a
car gets caught behind a slower one on lap 19, it
might be a good idea to come in. If the slower
car makes its pit stop on lap 19, the driver
behind might be able to complete two fast
laps before stopping.

△ Robert Kubica comes
into the pits to change
tires. Teams must
change tires at least
once during the race.

VARYING STRATEGY

There are lots of things that can force
a team's strategy to change during the
race. For example, a crash might mean
an early pit stop is a good idea. Or if it
stops raining, the drivers might have
to come in for new tires.

TECHNICAL DATA

Formula 1 cars must not do more
than 50 mph (80 km/h) in the pit
lane. In the tight Monaco pit lane,
this is reduced to 37 mph (60 km/h).

RACE SAFETY

With speeds of over 186 mph (300 km/h) and drivers racing each other just inches apart, Formula 1 looks like a dangerous sport. It can be, but there are lots of safety measures in place to make it as safe as possible.

TRACK SAFETY

Modern racetracks have lots of safety features. On corners where crashes are likely, there are run-off areas to allow the cars to slow down if they slide off. Gravel traps slow down the cars more quickly. When a crash does happen, officials wave flags to warn other drivers to take caution.

△ A crane lifts crashed cars out of the gravel at the European Grand Prix in Germany.

DRIVER SAFETY

If they are unlucky enough to crash, today's drivers have excellent protection:

- They wear fireproof Nomex suits and a HANS device (which stands for Head And Neck Support) to protect them from serious neck injuries.

- A safety cage stops drivers from being crushed in an accident. The sides are made of the same material as bulletproof vests, to stop splinters of metal from hitting the driver.

- The outer bodies of Formula 1 cars are designed to crumple in an accident, absorbing the force of the crash.

△ The outer body of Robert Kubica's car completely crumpled when he crashed at the Canadian Grand Prix in 2007. The safety cage surrounding his cockpit meant that Kubica escaped unharmed.

TECHNICAL DATA

Racecar drivers' Nomex suits would allow them to survive for 11 seconds in temperatures of 1,544°F (840°C). That's hotter than some volcanic lava!

RACING AROUND THE WORLD

As the Formula 1 teams travel the world, they visit lots of different kinds of racetracks. Some are old racing circuits layered in history. Others are ultra-modern tracks built in the last few years.

STREET CIRCUITS

Street circuits are racetracks that are also used as public roads (although not while the races are happening!). The most famous street circuit is Monaco. The newest is in Singapore, where the drivers face the added challenge of driving under floodlights!

▽ *The difficult Monaco Grand Prix is raced along the streets of Monte Carlo.*

◁ The new Shanghai International Circuit hosted the first ever Chinese Grand Prix in 2004.

PURPOSE-BUILT TRACKS

Today, most Formula 1 races take place on purpose-built tracks. Generally, these tracks are the safest. If cars run off the track, they slide safely to a halt instead of crashing into a wall. There are also places for spectators to sit or get something to eat.

THE KING OF TRACK DESIGN

Many of Formula 1's newest racetracks have been designed by Hermann Tilke. Tilke has designed racetracks in Malaysia, Bahrain, China, and Turkey. As he is also working on at least four more new circuits, Tilke really is the king of track design!

TECHNICAL DATA

GRAND PRIX VENUES, 2009

1	Australian GP	Melbourne
2	Malaysian GP	Kuala Lumpur
3	Chinese GP	Shanghai
4	Bahrain GP	Sakhir
5	Spanish GP	Catalunya
6	Monaco GP	Monte Carlo
7	Turkish GP	Istanbul
8	British GP	Silverstone
9	German GP	Hockenheim
10	Hungarian GP	Budapest
11	European GP	Valencia
12	Belgian GP	Spa-Francorchamps
13	Italian GP	Monza
14	Singapore GP	Singapore
15	Japanese GP	Suzuka
16	Brazilian GP	Sao Paulo
17	Abu Dhabi GP	Abu Dhabi

GLOSSARY

aerodynamics
Flow of air over and around an object.

analyze
Arrive at an understanding or explanation for something.

bhp
Short for brake horsepower, a way of measuring how powerful an engine is. The more bhp an engine has, the more powerful it is.

carbon fiber
A strong, wear-resistant material made of thin strands of carbon stuck together with glue.

closed circuits
Racetracks that are open only to race cars and are usually specially designed with driver and spectator safety in mind.

curbs
Raised sections at the side of a racetrack.

debut
Making a first appearance.

engineers
People who use science and technology to solve mechanical problems.

flying lap
A lap in which the car is already going as fast as it possibly can when it crosses the start line.

fuel consumption
The amount of fuel used to cover a set distance.

Grand Prix
A Formula 1 race.

grooved
With narrow tracks cut in.

km/h
Short for kilometers per hour.

mph
Short for miles per hour.

pole position
First place on the starting grid, the position awarded to the fastest qualifier.

race pace
A speed at which a car would be driven during a race.

reliability
A word used to describe something that is dependable, for example, a car that does not break down easily.

spectators
The people watching a race.

technology
The use of science for practical purposes, such as making a car go faster.

STAR DRIVERS

LEWIS HAMILTON

Born: January 7, 1985
Nationality: British

In 2007, Hamilton started his career with the best **debut** season ever, finishing second. He went one better in 2008, winning by just one point.

FELIPE MASSA

Born: April 25, 1981
Nationality: Brazilian

In 2008, Massa emerged as Ferrari's lead driver. His battle with Hamilton for the world championship excited racing fans everywhere.

ROBERT KUBICA

Born: December 7, 1984
Nationality: Polish

Behind the pack-leading McLarens and Ferraris, BMW Sauber's Kubica was the best driver of the 2008 season. He won the Canadian Grand Prix.

FERNANDO ALONSO

Born: July 27, 1981
Nationality: Spanish

Alonso was the youngest ever champion when he won at age 24 in 2005. Lewis Hamilton beat this record in 2008, winning at the age of just 23.

KIMI RÄIKKÖNEN

Born: October 17, 1979
Nationality: Finnish

Champion in 2007 by a single point. His greatest drive ever was probably in 2005, when he won the Japanese Grand Prix after starting 17th on the grid.

SEBASTIAN VETTEL

Born: July 3, 1987
Nationality: German

In 2007, Vettel became the youngest-ever points scorer. At the U.S. Grand Prix he stood in for Robert Kubica, who was injured, and finished eighth.

WEB SITES

www.formula1.com
The home site of the Formula 1 organization, this is an excellent place to keep up with what's going on during the racing season. It also details where each race will be held, including maps of the tracks. There are very good sections on understanding the sport, current teams and drivers, and a Hall of Fame with information about every Formula 1 world champion.

www.fia.com
The web site of the Fédération Internationale de l'Automobile (International Automobile Federation), which regulates most forms of motorsports—including Formula 1. The site is a good way to keep up with the current points standings and the racing calendar.

www.autosport.com
An excellent magazine site for all kinds of motorsport, especially Formula 1. Want to know what Lewis Hamilton thinks about the next race, or who's having tire problems in practice? This is the place to find out. Great for up-to-date news and current interviews.

INDEX